A HORSE WITHOUT A CARRIAGE

Love and Marriage Through the Ages

Martin Horrocks

EDGE EDITIONS

www.ituri.co.uk

CONTENTS

PREFACE...3

1 THAT FLASH OF LIGHTNING...4

2..LOVE AND MARRIAGE...12

3 LOVE AND LOSS...18

4 HEAVEN IS IN THOSE LIPS...24

5..ROMANCE AND REALITY...30

6 WHATEVER LOVE IS...37

7 GRIEF AND AFTER...43

PUBLICATION DATA...50

PREFACE

The idea of marrying for love is relatively recent. For most of history marriages were arranged or agreed for strictly practical reasons – economic, political, dynastic. Any connection between love and marriage was purely coincidental.

Even more recent – a product of the last fifty years, in fact – is the common belief that love can find fulfilment in any number of relationships as well as marriage. Perhaps the only oddity now is not to have a relationship.

'Love and marriage, love and marriage
Go together like a horse and carriage' *

Not any more they don't. This 1955 song continues:

'Dad was told by mother
You can't have one, you can´t have none
You can't have one without the other'

Nowadays oh yes he can!

*Songwriters: James Van Heusen / Sammy Cahn
Love And Marriage lyrics © Warner/Chappell Music Inc, Imagem Music Inc

CHAPTER ONE: THAT FLASH OF LIGHTNING

The French, as usual, have a word for it: they speak of a 'coup de foudre' (a bolt of lightning). Our expression in English – 'love at first sight' – is pretty pithy too, and goes back centuries. How much more exciting than building a relationship over weeks or months! But love at first sight, that flash of recognition when all our hopes cohere before our eyes – does it actually exist?

It is a concept that transcends cultures and centuries. It appears in Hindi love poems and in ancient Greece, where it was known as 'theia mania' (madness of the gods). Victims were pierced in the heart by arrows from Eros (Cupid). The phrase was used by Christopher Marlowe in his poem *Hero and Lysander* (1598):

Who ever lov'd, that lov'd not at first sight?

The line was picked up by Shakespeare in *As You Like It*, believed to have been written the following year, who gives it to the shepherdess Phebe as a quote. Incidentally, Marlowe's poem ends with a wise observation:

Where both deliberat, the love is slight,

Who ever lov'd, that lov'd not at first sight?

It's tempting to argue that when there's a word or words for it in many cultures, it must describe some sort of reality. And then we think of unicorns and mermaids, which undeniably don't exist. Even so, 'love at first sight' is such a common feeling that it's unlikely to describe nothing. But what does it describe?

The experience was unbeatably expressed in the Rogers and Hammerstein musical *South Pacific*:

Some enchanted evening, you may see a stranger,

You may see a stranger across a crowded room,

And somehow you know, you know even then,

That somehow you'll see her again and again.

Real life as well as romantic literature often confronts us with those who 'knew at once'. Few, however, follow through as quickly as actress Holly Matthews, then in her early twenties. She and the man who became her husband, Ross Blair, clicked instantly at a London promotional event. She moved the next day to Coventry to be with him. In 2012 they married, but the story has no happy ending. Just five years later Ross died from brain cancer.

One of the theatre's most famous love matches, that of Sir Laurence Olivier and Vivien Leigh, began with a flash of instant and mutual attraction. Both were married to other people at the time. Love at first sight, however, knows no boundaries.

Freed from the requirement of making dynastic marriages, even royalty can let its fancy fall where it may. Prince Harry was asked when he knew Meghan

Markle was the one. 'When did I know? From the very first time we met.' In loving an actress Harry is continuing an aristocratic tradition from the era of Edwardian stage-door-Johnnies and earlier. It had reached its apogee when Rosie Boot the Gaiety Girl became Rose, Marchioness of Headfort. A contemporary example is Allison Langer, the *Baywatch* babe (after the TV show), now Countess of Devon. By marrying a woman of mixed race Harry is following in the footsteps of Viscount Weymouth, heir to Longleat, who married Emma McQuiston of part-Nigerian origin.

We are less likely to fall in love at first sight with an ugly person than a beautiful one. Partly this is old-fashioned lust, but it is also due, as psychologist Aaron Ben-Zeev explains, to the 'attractiveness halo': what is beautiful is assumed to be good. The attribution may be quite wrong, but it may still yield intense love. If we're lucky this romantic intensity will last for years operating alongside romantic profundity drawn from shared activities and interests as well as feelings.

Ben-Zeev distinguishes these two dimensions of love with the telling though rather alarming example. A study discovered that if someone we're head over heels for invites us for coffee, the intense emotion is almost as much as saving a child from a car accident! However, in the case of our attractive coffee companion the emotion lasted for twenty minutes; with the child more than five hours (cited in a *Psychology Today* blog). Love at first sight can be the basis for profound love, according to

Ben-Zeev, provided that characteristics revealed later enhance, or at least don't contradict, the initial impression.

As we might expect, the impact of beauty decreases as we get to know the other person better and more important characteristics emerge. More surprisingly, despite women commonly asking for a GSOH (good sense of humour) in a partner, wittiness is also said to be of less importance as a relationship develops.

The reality of love at first sight received strong experimental support with the finding that advanced computer algorithms can't predict those who will be uniquely attracted to each other. The programs can determine who is desirable and how much someone would desire others – who's hot and who's not – but not whether two people will actually click. The findings were published in the journal *Psychological Science*.

'A relationship is more than the sum of its parts. There is a shared experience that happens when you meet someone that can't be predicted beforehand,' said Samantha Joel, a University of Utah psychology professor and lead author of the study.

The researchers used data from two samples of speed daters, who filled in questionnaires about more than one hundred traits and preferences and then met in a series of four-minute dates. Afterwards, the participants rated their interactions, indicating level of interest in and sexual attraction to each person they met.

'We found we cannot anticipate how much individuals will uniquely desire each other in a speed-dating context with any meaningful level of accuracy,' said Joel. 'I thought that out of more than one hundred predictors, we would be able to predict at least some portion of the variance. I didn't expect we would find zero.'

Paul W. Eastwick of the University of California, a co-author, said: 'Romantic desire may well be more like an earthquake, involving a dynamic and chaos-like process, than a chemical reaction involving the right combination of traits and preferences. It may be that we never figure it out, that it is a property we can never get at because it is simply not predictable.'

All of which is bad news for dating websites, who often claim that attraction between two people can be predicted from the right combination of traits and preferences. It seems that for now, and perhaps for always, there is no substitute for that jolt of electricity across a crowded room.

Romantics can also take heart from a *Health and Science* magazine report that the first few minutes of a meeting is predictive of the relationship's future success. Indeed, a person's attractiveness is determined in as little as 0.13 of a second, although this can hardly be other than lust. And lust is, after all, a necessary condition of a successful sexual/romantic relationship – a necessary but not sufficient condition.

Therefore lust at first sight, although a different animal, isn't disconnected. When we supposedly fall in love with an image, this is driven by lust or desire. Footballer David Beckham, who fell for Posh Spice when watching the Spice Girls on television, probably wasn't thinking about Victoria's qualities of mind or her aesthetic skills in dress designing. Nor before she met him was Vivien Leigh (mentioned earlier) likely to have been thinking about Sir Laurence Olivier's acting when she announced: 'That's the man I'm going to marry.'

The late politician Sir John Biggs-Davison is even said to have fallen in love with the woman who became his wife from her photograph on a grand piano. He was lucky. Little can be reliably concluded from a photo, especially a professionally taken one, which presents the person the photographer wants us to see; even less in the era of digital tweaking with Photoshop.

Admiring someone we've not met may create a willingness to love but, in contrast to love at first sight, it can't sensibly be called love. Interviews with entertainment personalities are the least likely way to discover what a person is really like. These celebrity interviews follow a well established formula in which journalist and subject are in unspoken alliance, usually with a public relations officer in tow, to create a carefully crafted image. The celebrities stress how normal they are and how their families come first. Neither may be true. The accompanying pictures almost inevitably have been digitally improved. Underneath the 'girl next door' or 'bloke down the pub' smile, the celebrity may be a ruthlessly ambitious, demanding prima donna who neglects family and children in pursuit of career.

Of course, some celebrities are normal and nice, and put their families first – but we can't tell who they are from press or TV interviews. It hardly matters. At least Sir John Biggs-Davison moved in the same social circles as the girl on the piano top and got to meet her. For most of us and notwithstanding the film *Notting Hill* – where a humble book-seller and an A-list film star meet accidentally and fall in love – our chances of more than a casual encounter with a celebrity are remote.

A striking case of willingness to love is that of the Russian novelist Ivan Turgenev. As a young man, he fell for the opera singer Pauline Viardot in 1843 after hearing her sing in the *The Barber of Seville*. The effect on Turgenev was lifelong. He engineered a meeting with the married Viardot, as a consequence of which he spent the rest of his life in love with her. Turgenev, who never married, followed her around Europe. The nature of their relations isn't clear. At one stage, he was living in the same house as the singer and her husband. The Villa Viardot at Bougival near Paris was the novelist's gift to his love.

Fandom is the harmless form of willingness to love. The poster on the bedroom wall, the shrieks and cries, the knickers thrown onto the stage – the fan then grows up and settles for life in the real world. In rare cases admiration for someone we haven't met becomes a chronic delusional disorder called De Clerambault's Syndrome, or erotomania. Vividly, it's also known as Old Maid's Insanity. Equally, sufferers may direct their attentions to people they know but who haven't returned their interest in any way; may even be unaware of the situation. Stalking, while not always delusional, can be a manifestation of De Clerambault's Syndrome.

The condition affects mainly but not exclusively women. Sufferers fancy themselves in love with an unattainable individual, typically older and of higher social status, or a celebrity, whom they may never have met or who may be married – or even dead. Against all the evidence sufferers are convinced that the other party secretly loves them.

Dr Frank Tallis describes how sensible, married 'Megan', a mid-forties lawyer's clerk, fell for her dentist, 'Dr Verma' (*The Incurable Romantic, and Other Unsettling Revelations*, 2018). She could 'see it in his eyes' that the married dentist felt the same. Except that to him, Megan was just another patient. She began stalking Dr Verma, phoning the surgery and then his home; standing outside the house. The more the dentist failed to respond, the more she was convinced that he was fighting his feelings for her. Medication had no effect. Eventually – and after the dentist had moved with his family to Dubai to escape her attentions – Megan experienced an epiphany. 'I know, I know,' she said, accepting that her imagined love could never be.

Dutch stalker Gert van der Graaf seems to have been not at all delusional in his pursuit of the Abba singer, Agnetha Faltskog, in the late-Nineties. Obsessed with her since childhood, he made numerous trips to Sweden to be close to his idol. Eventually he bought a house on the island of Ekero, where Agnetha was living in seclusion. From there it wasn't difficult to bring about a 'chance' meeting when she was out walking.

What followed was one of the weirdest episodes in the singer's life. She was going through a difficult patch in her personal life. Instead of politely acknowledging him and moving on, she was friendly to this stranger – and a sexual relationship followed. It lasted two years. Finally, Agnetha realised what Gert was about. She broke up the relationship, at which point Gert resumed stalking her. Agnetha now felt trapped and scared. After she made a humiliating court appearance, Gert was banned from contacting her and deported to the Netherlands. The orders eventually expired but, for whatever reason, he seems to have caused no more trouble in Agnetha's life.

The Van der Graaf affair shows what can happen when the invisible wall between celebrity and fan is breached.

CHAPTER TWO: LOVE AND MARRIAGE

The Church of England's Book of Common Prayer speaks plainly about the purposes of marriage:

First, 'for the procreation of children, to be brought up in the fear and nurture of the Lord ...'

Second, 'as a remedy against sin, and to avoid fornication; that such person as have not the gift of continency might marry, and keep themselves undefiled members of Christ's body.'

Third, 'for the mutual society, help, and comfort, that the one ought to have of the other ...'

This book dating from 1662 is still in use today (as one of several forms of worship), yet for most people its precepts could hardly be further from the understanding of marriage in the age of divorced parents, gay parents, transgender parents, single parents and non-parents (couples who choose not to have children).

The Book of Common Prayer, or BCP, held sway for centuries in England and, in various forms, around the English-speaking world. The purposes of marriage that it specified represented ideals, however often parishioners fell short, that most today hardly recognise and certainly don't accept. Only the third purpose – mutual support – has much traction now.

The idea that only the married may have children is long gone, as is the proposition that the primary purpose of marriage is to have children. Modern marriage has room for those who elect not to have children. Fornication isn't the sin it once was, or perhaps not a sin at all. As long as no one is hurt or exploited, call it experience.

The idea of continence (chastity) as a 'gift' seems ludicrous today. It's something one may choose, but it's neither better nor worse than its alternative. Help, comfort and companionship retain their attraction.

The word 'love' is missing from that set of precepts, although it occurs towards the end of the BCP service in a prayer. Love, however, is the driver of modern relationships. In the modern West, a loveless union is seen as wrong and a fraud on any children who follow. For much of the rest of the world, a love match is a luxury. Practical considerations rule the day.

A glance at how things were leaves no room for doubt about how fortunate we are with modern society's direction of travel.

The lack of effective contraception meant that children were the inevitable consequence of most marriages, whether wanted or not. Except for the wealthy who could farm out their childcare, multiple children tied women to the home leading to unfulfilled lives and depriving society at large of their brains and economic contributions. Matters began to change in the Thirties with barrier methods more effective than the condom. In the early Sixties the Pill finally gave women reproductive freedom, albeit at some long-term health risk, leading to today's perception of having children as a matter of choice.

The lack of effective contraception produced the spectres of the 'fallen woman' and the 'man who had to get married'. To avoid these fates vast numbers of women, presumably most, and large numbers of men went to their weddings as virgins. While this can be idealised as romantic, the practical effects were potentially serious. With no previous experience of each other, or anyone else, it was impossible for the couple to know whether they would be sexually compatible. They might discover too late that they weren't. Any relationship counsellor will testify that sexual mismatch can destroy a union that otherwise ticks all the boxes.

Whether or not the marriage worked, most couples were stuck with it. Divorce was impossible except for the rich, who could obtain an act of parliament dissolving the marriage. Others survived in misery, the household strife doing no service to the children. As well as the difficulty of obtaining it, divorce came with a stigma. Doubtless much of it can be traced back to that prayer book precept of children to be brought up 'in the fear and nurture of the Lord', for which a stable household with two parents was considered necessary.

Divorce could spell social ruin – another reason why it was relatively rare even among those who could afford it. Respectable wives feared 'fast' divorcees on the loose. From a later period, the 1934 film *The Gay Divorcee* ('gay' in the original sense) was to be called *The Gay Divorce*. The studio changed the title because, morally speaking, there should be no such thing a 'gay divorce'.

Matters improved gradually from the mid-19th century. The Matrimonial Causes Act, 1857, made divorce more widely available, with adultery as the ground for dissolution. Women faced a greater burden of proof than men, an inequity put right with the Matrimonial Causes Act, 1923, following the social upheaval of the First World War. Another act with the same name, that of 1937, added three further grounds for divorce beyond adultery (cruelty, desertion, insanity). However, only with the Divorce Reform Act, 1969 was it possible to divorce one's partner at will, in the sense of dissolving the marriage without their agreement. This act also replaced the idea of a guilty party with that of 'irretrievable breakdown' of the marriage with neither side to blame.

When I was a child in the 1950s, there were just two divorced individuals within my family's circle of acquaintance. It was a matter of (non-censorial) comment. No one would be commenting now.

Following the 1969 act (consolidated by the Matrimonial Causes Act, 1973), the divorce rate has soared leading to healthier relationships and happier homes, but with the inevitable remarriages and new unions producing today's range of 'blended families', half-siblings, step-children and the rest. A house with a mum and a dad may still be, as many survey findings suggest, the best bet for children, but equally they may thrive with a single parent, divorced parents or same-sex parents.

What ultimately matters is love, not who or how many are giving it.

Marriage back in the day was the only career open to almost all women above the level of domestic service. The alternative was permanent aunthood, perpetual virginity and a life of embroidery and good works. Marriage was a must when it could be got, and love if it happened was a bonus. The heroines of Jane Austen's novels (chapter five) are lucky in love, albeit with a keen eye on issues of money, rank and title. In the higher tiers of society where land was involved, men also were limited in their roles. The rule of primogeniture meant that the eldest son took all, leaving the others to survive as best they could. Often they went into the church or the armed forces.

In Austen's time, the early 19th century, women had some say in whom they married. In earlier periods heiresses were traded for political or economic reasons. Men of position often needed to marry for dynastic reasons. Henry VIII married Catherine of Aragon after her first husband, Henry's elder brother and heir to the throne, died; he committed to marry his fourth and least successful wife, Anne of Cleves, without having met her. The 'Flanders mare' was proof that before photography portraits could lie. Medieval 'courtly love' (chapter three), existing in the mind, was a way to sublimate urges that arranged marriages didn't satisfy.

Although the idea of love and marriage going together as naturally as a horse and carriage is a relatively modern one, the idea of love matches certainly isn't. We remember great lovers of life and legend: Dante and Beatrice (chapter three), Helen of Troy and Paris, Lancelot and Guinevere, Antony and Cleopatra, Abelard and Heloise (all chapter four), Elizabeth and Darcy (chapter five). Outside romantic fiction, many love affairs ended badly. Perhaps that helped reconcile people to their humdrum, more-or-less-all-right marriages. Resigning crowns and losing worlds for love weren't reliable guides in reality. How lucky we are that in the present day we can marry whom we like, provided he or she will have us.

CHAPTER THREE: LOVE AND LOSS

The classic among classics of romantic love is that of Dante and Beatrice. The 13th century poet Dante Alighieri loved Beatrice Portinari from when he was aged nine. He wrote in *Vita Nuova*: 'Behold, a deity stronger than I; who coming, shall rule over me.' And yet they hardly met – twice as children and once as adults, the last time by chance in a Florence street. This was the meeting imagined in the famous painting by Henry Holiday almost six hundred years later. The scene is the riverside. Dante stands several feet away from Beatrice, staring at her. Beatrice, accompanied by two women, looks resolutely ahead. It could be a snapshot of strangers passing in the street, but we have to assume that moments later they talked.

Dante's family had social status in Florence, and he himself was heavily involved in the politics of the Italian city state and the tussle between the Papacy and the Holy Roman Emperor. Beatrice's father was a banker, as was her husband. Thus politics meets economics, or rather did not meet in the poet's case. Dante supported the Guelph movement, rulers of the city and supporters of the Papacy. The young Dante fought in the Battle of Capaldino (1289), when the Guelphs prevailed over the Ghibbelines from surrounding states, who supported the emperor. Two factions among the Guelphs, the white and the black, fell out. The blacks took over, and Dante was among several prominent whites to be exiled.

One year after the battle, Beatrice died aged just twenty-four. Dante had had no relationship with Beatrice, whose nickname was Bice, in the modern sense. He admitted that she was 'la gloriosa donna della mia mente' (the glorious lady of my mind). This does not make his love any the less real. And for whatever reason, political or social, the mind was where it stayed. Dante was realist enough to know it wasn't to be: despite his idealised feelings for Beatrice he married someone else two years before Beatrice married.

She appears not only in *Vita Nuova* (1295) but also some years later in *Paradiso* (Heaven), the final part of *The Divine Comedy*. In *Vita Nuova* Beatrice is described as 'most kind' and 'blessed'. In *The Divine Comedy* she is Dante's guide through Heaven. She is 'maternal, radiant and comforting'. Together they meet Thomas Aquinas and other venerated Christians. Meanwhile, Dante's wife, Gemma di Manetto Donati, isn't mentioned in any of his poems.

Vita Nuova is a celebration of the ideal of courtly love. No wonder Dante was drawn to the genre. He had been promised in marriage aged twelve, when he was already nurturing his feelings for Beatrice.

If love at first sight is a universal idea, it is matched by that of thwarted or unrequited love, where the lover bravely accepts what he or she can't have. We don't know what Beatrice thought about Dante, if anything. Perhaps verses from Handel's 1728 opera *Tolomeo* applied to him:

Did you not hear my lady

Go down the garden singing?

Blackbird and thrush were silent

To hear the alleys ringing ...

Though I am nothing to her,

Though she must rarely look at me,

Though I can never woo her

I'll love her till I die.

These lines, in the 1928 English-language translation by Arthur Somervell, became a huge hit with choirs and soloists alike, reinforcing the romance of love that isn't to be.

We don't know whether the nine-year-old Dante setting eyes on Beatrice experienced love at first sight in the literal sense. In any case, can children know romantic love in a meaningful way? Of Helen Beck's love at first sight for the actor Peter Cushing there is no doubt. In convincing words, written to a friend and reprinted by Peter in his autobiography, the woman who became his first and only wife tells how it happened. She had been engaged to replace an actress in a show in which he was appearing; then:

... From the stage-door stepped a vision, and my heart skipped a beat ... Tall and lean, a pale, almost haggard face, with astonishingly large, blue eyes: on his head an old grey velvet hat, with a hole between the dents of its crown, a jacket beyond description and repair, spotless white shirt badly frayed at cuffs and collar, a pair of once dark blue corduroy trousers, most of the nap long since worn away through constant wear, down-at-heel shoes of grey suede ... There was an aura about this 'beloved vagabond'. His hands told me he was either a musician or an artist* ... I knew I would love him for the rest of my days – and beyond ... (*Peter Cushing: An Autobiography*, 1986)

*Helen was correct. Peter Cushing was a considerable painter as well as an actor.

Noteworthy here is that Helen's perceptions transcend 'lust at first sight'. Yes, he is tall and lean with 'astonishingly large, blue eyes'. But she correctly infers that he is a loner in need of looking after, and no mere jobbing actor but an artist as well. Peter returned her feelings. Theirs was to be a marriage of great devotion, followed for him by twenty-three years of bereavement.

Peter Cushing was a more considerable actor than his Hammer horror films roles suggest, with many theatres appearances and a tour of Australia with Sir Laurence Olivier and his party. Born in 1913, Peter tried his luck in Hollywood as the Second World War approached. Good parts were coming through when he felt the need to return to wartime Britain, which after a hazardous sea crossing he managed. He performed for the troops with ENSA (Entertainment National Service Association). It was at one of these touring productions – Noel Coward's *Private Lives* – that he met Helen Beck.

She was born in Saint Petersburg of an English father and a Swedish/Polish mother. The family was well to do, but that comfort disappeared when they had to flee Russia with the Bolshevik revolution. She became a showgirl at the prestige end of the work, as one of C.B. Cochrane's Young Ladies. Helen was eight years older than Peter and a divorcee. He was a bachelor. Helen had breathing problems from their earliest days, and was to die of an asthmatic condition aged sixty-five.

The couple were obsessed with each other. He called her 'divine'; she declared that he had the greatest 'courage, integrity (and seven other listed qualities)' of all the men and women she had known. There was a miscarriage, but otherwise no children. Peter's autobiography was published fifteen years after her death, and is unmistakably written by himself, not ghost-written. It is dedicated to Helen, 'who made all things possible'. More than that, it is a memorial to her. He ends his story in the year of her death 'since my life as I knew and loved it ended with the passing of my beloved wife Helen'.

His life had more than two decades to run. He never married again, dying in 1994, aged eighty-one. In interviews he often expressed the view that he was marking time until he was reunited with Helen. But he knew he had to carry on because she told him in a letter she left:

... let the sun shine in your heart. Do not pine for me, my beloved Peter, because that will cause unrest. Do not be hasty to leave this world, because you will not go until you have lived the life you have been given. AND REMEMBER we will meet again when the time is right ... This is my promise ...'

Peter adds as the final sentence of the book: 'I have been doubtful many times about many things during my life, but of this I have no doubt – no doubt whatsoever.'

Is fidelity after death to be admired or pitied? How is such an attitude to be accommodated within the notion that grief moves in stages before emerging into some sort of sunlit upland? And what makes a sunlit upland?

CHAPTER FOUR: HEAVEN IS IN THOSE LIPS

... a feeling that lovers have always known. It was Christopher Marlowe in his late 16th century play *Doctor Faustus* who found the words:

Was this the face that launched a thousand ships,

And burnt the topless towers of Ilium?

Sweet Helen, make me immortal with a kiss.

Her lips suck forth my soul: see where it flies.

Come, Helen, come, give me my soul again.

Here will I dwell for heaven is in those lips,

And all is dross that is not Helena. [Act 5, Scene 1]

The mythological Helen of Troy stands forever as the ideal of female beauty. Faustus has sold his soul to the Devil in exchange for twenty-four years of magical powers and all the world's knowledge. At the end of the period Faust will go to Hell. As the time draws near the terrified Faust summons Helen, but neither she nor anyone else can save him.

Helen was the daughter of Zeus, king of the gods. She was the wife of King Menelaus of Sparta. Her abduction by her lover Paris precipitated the Trojan War and eventually the fall of Troy. The story of the war and its sequel, Odysseus's ten-year journey home, are told in Homer's *Iliad* and *Odyssey*. Troy finally fell after the Greeks built their famous Trojan Horse, stuffed with soldiers, which the curious Trojans fatally brought inside the city walls.

As with so many famous loves in life and legend, things ended badly for Helen and Paris. He was killed in the war and Menelaus, reunited with Helen, was poised to kill her before finding himself disarmed by her beauty. The surviving texts are unclear about Helen's ultimate fate, ranging from living happily ever after to being hanged.

Troy was traditionally thought to be as mythological as the Trojan Way. However, the German archaeologist Heinrich Schliemann in 1870 unearthed the remains of the city. It is now a Unesco world heritage site.

Britain's supreme love myth is that of Lancelot and Guinevere. The setting, King Arthur's court at Camelot, may be better described as semi-mythological. The tales of Arthur and his court are widely thought to be legends derived from the life of an actual Romano-British chief; Camelot is located at various sites in the West of England.

Sir Lancelot du Lac falls in love with Guinevere, who is Arthur's queen. The lovers cause a civil war and the collapse of Camelot. Many versions of the tale exist. In the best known, they atone by becoming a hermit and a nun respectively.

The Arthurian legends date from the 12th century, several hundred years after the possible existence of Camelot. The tale of Tristan and Iseult (Isolde) is from the same period and is connected to the legends. Tristan, a Cornish knight, and the Irish princess Iseult fall in love after swallowing a love potion. Iseult is the wife of Tristan's uncle, King Mark. In many versions of the tale, it ends badly for the adulterous pair with Tristan being killed by Mark.

In the real world, things are no better. The most famous lovers in the Western canon are Antony and Cleopatra. Antony's choice was brilliantly expressed by John Dryden in the title of his 1678 play: *All for Love, or the World Well Lost.*

Antony was one of the rulers of the Roman Empire; Cleopatra reigned as queen of Egypt from 51 to 30 BCE. Far from being the doe-eyed sybarite memorably portrayed by Amanda Barrie in *Carry On Cleo* (1964), she was politically ambitious with expansionary aims. Before Antony, she had dallied with Julius Caesar and bore him a son. She sided with the faction led by Antony and Octavian (the future emperor Augustus) against Brutus and Cassius, the principal assassins of Julius Caesar. Antony visited Alexandria, Cleopatra's capital, in 41 and was so charmed that he stayed for several months. Twins were the result. He returned four years later – and stayed (producing another child), exiling himself from the seat of imperial power.

Rome was wary of Cleopatra's political ambitions. Relations between Antony and Octavian broke down, leading to the sea battle of Actium in 31. This set the lovers on a course for disasters and death. Cleopatra's ships joined Antony's, but at the height of the battle her fleet deserted. Antony followed with his ships, handing victory to Octavian. It would not now be long before Octavian came to get them. He invaded Egypt the following year. Antony's army deserted him.

The lovers' last year has become the stuff of legend. It is told by Plutarch in his *Life of Antony*, an account that may or may not have been heroically embellished:

Antony felt, rightly, that Cleopatra had failed him with her desertion. She feared revenge, and sent a message falsely claiming she was dead. Overcome with grief, he stabbed himself in the stomach. He learnt too late that she was alive. He had himself carried to her and there died. Cleopatra evidently felt no need to join him in a double suicide. Her time came later after she had been captured by Octavian. She feared the humiliation of being taken to Rome and paraded in chains in his triumph. Somehow she tricked the guards, and killed herself with an asp (cobra) or toxic ointment. The asp legend is possibly not true. Death was not guaranteed with an asp bite; poison, if available, offered certainty.

If Antony and Cleopatra's was the most famous love affair of antiquity, that of Abelard and Heloise fills the role for the middle ages. The reputation is undeserved – more lust by Abelard and reluctant acquiescence by Heloise.

Abelard (c 1079-1142) was a brilliant philosopher and theologian. By his own admission he sought to seduce Heloise (1090?/1100-01 ?-1164) because she was the most famous woman scholar in France, fluent in Latin, Greek and Hebrew. He convinced Heloise's uncle and guardian Fulbert, with whom she lived, to let him move into the house in 1115 or 1116. They began an affair, with Abelard boasting about his conquest. A son was born. Heloise's birth date is highly uncertain. If the latest date is taken, she would have been fifteen – scandalous now and not then, but with the stigma of illegitimacy.

They married after an initially reluctant Heloise agreed. Fulbert, however, believed Abelard planned to leave Heloise. As a punishment, he hired thugs to castrate him. Abelard then became a monk at St Denis. Heloise, meanwhile, had been forced into a nunnery. She disliked monastic life and became a hermit. Her isolation was short. Followers flocked to the site near Nogent-sur-Seine, in Champagne, which developed into the Oratory of the Paraclete.

Abelard, whose fame was cemented with writing and debating, resumed contact with Heloise, by now an abbess, around 1129. She seems to have bowed to the inevitable in co-operating with Abelard in putting together the love letters and religious correspondence on which their fame rests. There are seven letters. He tells her that he never truly loved her, only lusted after her. Their relationship was a sin against God. Only Christ truly loved her. She sees marriage as contractual prostitution: 'I preferred love to wedlock, freedom to a bond.'

Abelard died in 1142. After burial elsewhere his remains were later brought to the Oratory of the Paraclete. Heloise was buried alongside him in 1163. Such is their lasting fame that their bones were moved several times. They now apparently lie in Pere Lachaise cemetery, Paris. (The identity of the bones has been disputed.)

The strange relationship of Abelard and Heloise was either an on again-off again love affair or abuse by the egotist and control freak Abelard of Heloise at a time when women were wholly dependent on men. Perhaps even the participants didn't know which it was.

These lovers in life and legend are idealised women. The danger of carrying this too literally into real life is set out by Jonathan Swift in his poem *The Lady's Dressing Room*. A young man, Strephon, steals into the dressing room of his goddess, Celia. He is repulsed by the stinks and smells he finds there. In unsparing couplets we, like Strephon, encounter

A paste of composition rare,/Sweat, dandruff, powder, lead and hair;

or

The basin takes whatever comes/The scrapings of her teeth and gums,

and so on and so on.

Thus finishing his grand survey,/Disgusted Strephon stole away/Repeating in his amorous fits,/Oh! Celia, Celia, Celia shits!

The famous last line would not have shocked the first 1732 readers as it has those later. It isn't the final punchline. Swift uses a separate idea for his strong ending (see below). The poem may be read as a reminder that women are just as human as the men who put them on a pedestal. Furthermore, it's a bad idea to inquire into the artifice behind the glamour. The experience in Celia's dressing room makes 'wretched Strephon blind/To all the charms of female kind'.

He is needlessly denying himself. Swift concludes his poem:

Such order from confusion sprung,
Such gaudy tulips raised from dung.

CHAPTER FIVE: ROMANCE AND REALITY

Spoiler alert: This chapter has sections on the classic novels *Pride and Prejudice* and *The Woman in White*. If you don't wish to know the stories and how they end, stop reading at the titles in bold type and resume at the next bold sub-heading or the next chapter.

The novels of Jane Austen are mines of information about the customs of the late-Georgian period. They aren't modern reconstructions of what the past was thought to be like, but testimony from someone who was there. They are also evidence of how much of the English language has stayed the same and how much a few terms have changed meaning, sometimes dramatically. 'Sensation', for example, meant a slight feeling, not a huge one. 'Making love' and 'intercourse' are found widely in Jane's work but, as will be easily imagined, they aren't used in the modern sense!

Both terms have narrowed in recent times. In her day and much earlier, 'making love' meant making amorous approaches or being flirtatious. In general use it continued that way until after the Second World War and perhaps later; now it exclusively means having sex. 'Intercourse' for Jane simply meant communication between two or more individuals. 'Intercourse in the park' was a conversation, nothing more. 'Social intercourse' is just still possible today, although it's a brave person (or a pompous one) who uses the word. Without a qualifying adjective, it unavoidably means sex.

In Jane's most famous novel, *Pride and Prejudice*, published in 1813, it's clear from the first chapter that marriages weren't arranged at that time, at least in a formal sense. Mr Bennet, the father of five girls, tells his wife that he would assure the eligible incomer Mr Bingley 'of my hearty consent to his marrying which ever he chuses of the girls'.

Having heard of Bingley's large fortune – four or five thousand pounds a year – Mr Bennet would know the advantage of *any* daughter marrying a man so much above them in wealth. While marriages were no longer arranged in the medieval sense, a lover's choice was constrained by wealth or rank or both in all but the lowest tiers of society. The Bennet girls had uncles who were attorneys. On hearing this, Bingley's friend Mr Darcy remarks '… it must very materially lessen their chances of marrying men of any consideration in the world'.

Pride and Prejudice

Enough money could overcome such typical snobbery, as when Charlotte Lucas, a daughter of trade, marries Mr Collins, the heir to Longbourn. But in sentiments shocking to our modern understanding Darcy's cousin, Colonel Fitzwilliam – one of the good guys – tells Elizabeth Bennet that '… there are not many in my rank of life who can afford to marry without some attention to money' and again, 'Younger sons [like him] cannot marry where they like.' To which Elizabeth responds drily, 'Unless where they like women of fortune ...'

Mr Bingley is sweet on the eldest girl, Jane, leading one of his sisters to comment:

'I have an excessive regard for Jane Bennet, she is really a very sweet girl, and I wish with all my heart she were well settled. But with such a father and mother, and with such low connections, I am afraid there is no chance of it.'

Except he does marry her. Austen's novels are romances where her heroines marry and live happily ever after. Elizabeth wins the richest and noblest of them all, Mr Darcy. The romances are literary artefacts against the background where most matches were determined by money or rank – a reality that Austen continually stresses. It was especially advantageous for a man to marry a woman with property or income because all her assets became his upon marriage. Single women and widows kept theirs. This was the ancient doctrine of 'spousal unity', not overturned until the Married Women's Property Act of 1870 – a measure as momentous as the 'votes for women' act of 1918, for which it paved the way.

From the evidence of *Pride and Prejudice*, young women had just one trump card: the power of accepting or rejecting a marriage proposal. Parents might pressure – as Mrs Bennet does, unsuccessfully, with Elizabeth over Mr Collins's suit – but could not dictate. Mr Collins, disappointed in Elizabeth, then addresses himself to

Charlotte, who accepts him. The couple then apply to her parents for consent. Charlotte is twenty-seven. Her motive in accepting Mr Collins is entirely prudential, to use an Austen word:

Mr Collins, to be sure, was neither sensible [sensitive] nor agreeable; his society was irksome, and his attachment to her must be imaginary. But still he would be her husband. Without thinking highly either of men or matrimony, marriage had always been her object; it was the only provision for well-educated young women of small fortune, and however uncertain of giving happiness, must be their pleasantest preservative from want.

Who now or then will blame Charlotte in this age of limited opportunities for women?

Elizabeth later turns down Darcy when he calls on her unexpectedly, and with an agitated manner asks for her hand. She is staying with the now-married Collinses, so her parents are nowhere to be seen. When she accepts him it isn't, under the conventions of romantic fiction, for rank and fortune but because the social boor has redeemed himself.

In the real world Elizabeth, lacking the novelist's prevision that she would marry Darcy, was taking a risk in turning down Mr Collins. For almost all women of the period an unsuitable marriage was better than no marriage. The alternative was the stigma of spinsterhood, permanent aunthood and lifetime dependency in the family home. All of which was Jane

Austen's lot. One wonders how keenly she felt disappointment, if at all. Perhaps her career as a successful novelist allowed her to transcend such feelings.

Prudential considerations also applied to men. *The Lass of Richmond Hill* is a 1789 hit song that Jane Austen most likely knew. It remains popular today, expressing a noble sentiment:

I'd crowns resign

To call thee mine,

Sweet lass of Richmond Hill.

We'd like to think we would make such a sacrifice, but few did where money, rank or titles were concerned.

The Woman in White

Romantic fiction from Austen's time to the present requires the heroines to be chaste maidens and the heroes to be rich, titled or powerful *, yet the central characters in Wilkie Collins's *The Woman in White* (1860) are none of these things. Walter Hartright, the hero, has more important characteristics – courage and persistence – while Laura Fairlie, the heroine, is rare in Victorian romantic fiction in not going to the wedding bed a virgin. She is a widow, albeit one who endured a loveless and abusive marriage.

* nowadays add 'tall'. See how often that word is attached to the hero rather than 'middle height' or 'short' in contemporary romantic or mid-market novels!

The story opens when the hero Walter Hartright is employed to teach drawing to two young women at lonely Limmeridge House in Cumberland. One of them is Laura. The other is her half-sister, Marian Halcombe. Walter falls instantly for Laura. In his own words to the reader:

Think of her as you thought of the first woman who quickened the pulses within you that the rest of her sex had no art to stir. Let the kind, candid blue eyes meet yours, as they met mine, with the one matchless look which we both remember so well. Let her voice speak the music that you once loved best, attuned as sweetly to your ear as to mine. Let her footstep, as she comes and goes, in these pages, be like that other footstep to whose airy fall your own heart once beat time.

Despite Laura returning his feelings, Hartright is unable to prevent her being swept into a long-arranged marriage with the villainous Sir Percival Glyde. The story, now taken up by Marian Halcombe, records her impressions when Laura returns 'improved' from her honeymoon:

There is more colour, and more decision and roundness of outline in her face than there used to be; and her figure seems more firmly set, and more sure and easy in all its movements *than it was in her maiden days* [italics added].

It can't be love because the marriage was arranged and joyless. The plain suggestion is that sex is good for a woman, affecting not only mood (which everyone knows) but also physical movements. Can this be so, or is Collins indulging in a male dis-virgining fantasy? Or is the (fictitious) narrator, Miss Halcombe, exercising her own repressions?

Sir Percival has married Laura for her money. The relationship becomes sexless, evidenced by his remark that she will never have children. For us readers this restores Laura to something like her maiden state. After the baronet dies in a fire, Walter, Laura and Marian live chastely together. Eventually, after many vicissitudes Walter and Laura are free to marry. They live happily at Limmeridge with their baby son, supported by the ever-virgin Marian.

CHAPTER SIX: WHATEVER LOVE IS

Spoiler alert: This chapter has sections on the classic novels *The Tenant of Wildfell Hall* and *The Woman in White*. If you don't wish to know the stories and how they end, stop reading at the title in bold type and resume at the next chapter.

He first saw the girl who was to dominate the rest of his life across a crowded hotel room – but what is it that Howard Jenkins saw? Howard is the central figure – the 'hero' in inverted commas – in my novel *Everyman and the Beautiful People* (2017). He is neither short nor tall.

He is presentable but not handsome, competent but not exceptional. He is neither aristocratic nor working class. He is not from London or Grimsby but from Bristol.

Meg Denby, the girl on the other side of the room, is tall, beautiful and at twenty-two a famous actress and film star. She is the daughter of a lord, living in a Yorkshire mansion set amid its ancestral acres. Howard correctly intuits that she is also a genuinely nice person. But would he have shown the same compulsion to know her if she'd been a waitress at the event with a pretty face and a sympathetic manner? Hardly.

Howard is a reporter at a literary luncheon where Meg is a top-table guest. He seeks her afterwards, and her friendliness captivates him all the more. He pores over her press cuttings in the newspaper's library. He traces her to the house where she is visiting and speaks briefly on the phone. At first he is elated, then in despair.

He had done it. He had spoken to her – and he felt worse than ever. He had never had such a sense of rapport as he did with this girl. A few minutes earlier it had seemed that the exciting world of Meg Denby was within his grasp. Now it was over.

When he meets Meg again at a social event he is covering, he finds the guts to ask her to dance. She accepts. Howard mistakes simple friendliness for an expression of interest. Soon Meg has to leave Yorkshire for filming. Howard is consumed by envy. This is the late Sixties, the time of the 'Summer of Love', when the air was heavy with possibilities, none of it seeming to waft in his direction.

The London world of Meg Denby seemed completely inaccessible to Howard, and he wanted passionately to enter it. He imagined it as the world of artists, where creative people – writers, painters, musicians, sculptors, actors and directors – mingled, and fired one another with their ideas. He, meanwhile, sat in a miserable provincial flat pounding out attempt after attempt at a novel. The results were always dreadful.

He follows her to London. He writes and gets no reply. He leaves phone messages with the same result. Desperate, he presents himself at the film studio, insisting that a sceptical door-keeper send in a message. And then the impossible happens: Meg sends a friendly note in reply.*

Howard is what a later time would call stalking Meg. Unlike some cases of stalking mentioned in chapter one, he is not at all delusional. He's as prudential is his pursuit as any Jane Austen character. He desires not fame, fortune or rank but lifestyle. Is he in love with Meg or the life of glamour and the arts that she represents?

*Everyman and the Beautiful People. To read the continuing story: amazon.co.uk or amazon.com for the Kindle ebook edition, or ituri.co.uk for the printed edition in three parts.

The Tenant of Wildfell Hall

If proof is wanted of women's capacity to fall for rogues, it is to be found in Anne Bronte's *The Tenant of Wildfell Hall* (1848). Arthur Huntingdon is a handsome rake – debauched, sadistic and a leading light in a dissolute drinking circle. He has spent his way through much of his inherited fortune. The heroine Helen – the mysterious and beautiful 'Mrs Graham', the tenant of the title – loves him in the belief that she can save him from himself. She marries him despite warnings from her aunt and others.

Huntingdon is a bully. He grabs and holds on to Helen as she rides her horse. On another occasion, he seizes her portfolio of drawings, pocketing one that takes his fancy:

'Mr Huntingdon,' cried I, 'I insist upon having that back! It is mine, and you have no right to take it. Give it me, directly – I'll never forgive you if you don't!'

But the more vehemently he insisted, the more he aggravated my distress by his insulting gleeful laugh. At length, however, he restored it to me, saying –

'Well, well, since you value it so much, I'll not deprive you of it.'

Helen responded with spirit:

To show him how much I valued it I tore it in two and threw it into the fire.

When Huntingdon threatens to corrupt their four-year-old son, Helen leaves her husband with her brother's support. She takes up residence in a semi-derelict family property, Wildfell Hall, alone except for her son. A neighbouring farmer, the stolid Gilbert Markham, finally learns the secret of 'Mrs Graham'. After Huntingdon's death, true love finds the way, and Helen and Gilbert marry.

The Tenant of Wildfell Hall was a huge success upon publication. Mid-Victorian readers were both fascinated and shocked by Helen's spirit and independence at a time when women were expected to obey their husbands – and certainly not to leave them, come what may. For Helen to live alone at Wildfell Hall further outraged polite society. Critics latched on to what several called the 'coarseness' of the book, meaning that it depicted scenes of domestic (non-violent) abuse that were better left behind closed doors.

Later *The Tenant* fell from favour before being rediscovered in recent times as a feminist statement, an early blast of the trumpet for the rights of women.

Whatever love is, it doesn't have a single trigger like measles; its causes are multiple. In this chapter:

Howard's love for Meg is highly 'prudential'. He fell for the lifestyle first, then the person. Without the lifestyle he would doubtless have forgotten the person.

The religious Helen loves Arthur Huntingdon because it allows her the chance of saving him as well as being drawn to his roguish charms.

Gilbert slowly but steadily falls in love with the mysterious stranger. His and Helen's love becomes a true union of minds and bodies. It happens in real life, too

The Tenant of Wildfell Hall and The Woman in White

The plots of *The Tenant of Wildfell Hall* (above) and *The Woman in White* (see chapter five) have striking similarities, noteworthy in the Victorian era. Each features a strong, independent woman in the form of Helen Huntingdon (nee Lawrence) and Marian Halcombe respectively. The heroes, Gilbert Markham in *The Tenant* and Walter Hartwright in *WIW*, are middle class – a farmer and an artist respectively. They are beneath the women socially, but marry 'up' in true love matches. Neither Helen nor Laura Fairlie *(WIW)* is a virgin. They are widows who have emerged from abusive marriages. The way has to be cleared for the happy endings by the deaths of the first husbands. Divorce would detract from the purity of the heroines. It was in any case impossible when *The Tenant* was published for all except the very richest, and had only recently been made more widely available when *WIW* appeared. As well as their marital bliss, Gilbert and Walter both end up living in mansions – inherited by their wives.

CHAPTER SEVEN: GRIEF AND AFTER

Great love is inseparable sooner or later from great loss, through death, divorce, separation or the slow extinction of a union. Unrequitedness, where only one of two people fall in love, is another form of bereavement. Where death is concerned, our sense of loss depends on a host of factors including the age of the dead person, our relationship to him or her and the nature of the illness or accident. One of the revelations about death is that for the survivors it may bring out feelings they didn't know they had. Two sisters, for example, have been estranged for years, yet the survivor is totally unexpectedly grief-stricken.

The saying 'blood is thicker than water' is never more true than with death. We can suggest a 'sliding scale' of grief, with parents, children and grandchildren at the top, along with spouses (or partners) in successful marriages. Siblings come close behind. Aunts, uncles and cousins are next (when there has been frequent contact), with friends generally last. We feel sad for them all, but the intensity of our grief varies. When two of my near relations died within a year, I was amazed at how much more my sister's death affected me than did my first cousin's. I'd been close to both, but genetics seem to have been at work.

Seven stages of grief have been described by Dr David Delvin following a bereavement*:

Shock, disbelief, numbness

Denial

Panic

Anger

Guilt

Depression

Acceptance

*Web posting on netdoctor.co.uk

This time-tested model has its critics, but it continues to reflect the experience of many sufferers, including me. The bereaved move through these stages at different speeds. Stages may overlap, be experienced concurrently. Some people get stuck along the way and need help. They will hopefully come to see that despair is not what the loved one would want and the best way to honour the dead is to carry on with normal life. Moreover, they have what hundreds of thousands of their contemporaries lack and would love to have – life. To be permanently grief-bound is an insult to all who died before their time.

Acceptance is the final stage in the grieving process, but what does it mean? A survey found that eighteen months after the death of a spouse thirty-seven per cent of widowers and fifteen per cent of widows over sixty-five were found to be interested in dating. For many people the desire for romance never dies. Others want to be active socially without the burden and demands of a 'relationship'. Practical reasons point to finding a new partner – social life is mainly based on pairs, or singles groups that are way-stations to pairing off – but even so some, like the actor Peter Cushing (chapter three), having lost 'the one and only', don't wish to find another.

Does fidelity like Cushing's to the memory of a dead partner not count as one of the sunlit uplands of acceptance? It's not 'moving on' in the conventional sense, but if love finds sufficient nourishment in the mind, who is to brand that a failure?

Fidelity like this is far removed from the pragmatic, not to say utilitarian, approach of the anthropologist Margaret Mead, variously quoted as saying that every woman or every person has three loving relationships in them: in youth for sex; in middle age for security while raising children; in old age for companionship

One might point out that this is the profile of the typical successful marriage, but presumably Mead meant more than that. Her love life was colourful but didn't follow her own script. She was married three times, rapidly replacing one husband with the next, then lived for more than twenty years until her death in 1978 aged seventy-six with a woman – fellow anthropologist Rhoda

Metraux. Lily King's novel *Euphoria* (2014) brings together in a light disguise Mead and her second and third husbands.

Few are as open about the fear of being alone as actress and dancing star Debbie McGee, who was the partner then wife of the late magician Paul Daniels for thirty-eight years. Two years after Daniels died, Debbie, aged fifty-nine, announced that she was ready for love again. 'I don't want to be on my own for the rest of my life [she said]. I love male company, am full of energy and don't want to be stuck at home alone.'

For Constance Wood, a sixty-year-old artist and lecturer, the need for a plus-one at social events impelled her to try online dating three years after the death of her lawyer husband. 'I didn't want to be the only one on my own at dinners and parties any more,' Constance explained to the *Daily Mail*].

She soon fell for a smart and attractive man, Martin Petersen, with long silver hair and a trustworthy smile. Trouble was, 'Martin Petersen' didn't exist. The man Constance was looking at on the internet was someone whose identity had been stolen by a scammer – a victim of 'catfishing'. Using the fake identity, 'Martin Petersen' soon built up a relationship by email and telephone.

Constance eventually saw through the ruse before she handed over any money. Using Google matching technology, she then discovered that the pictures were of

Steve Bustin, an entirely innocent businessman whose images had been taken from Facebook and other web sources. The story doesn't end there, however. When challenged, the resourceful scammer even claimed that the pictures were truly of him and Steve had stolen *his* identity. 'I'm going to have him shut down,' he declared.

With the situation developing like a film script Constance began to wonder who was real and who wasn't. Finally, the truth came out on top and 'Martin Petersen' disappeared defeated. With a happy ending worthy of the movies, Constance met Steve Bustin in person. He was as charming as she had hoped. He was also married – and gay.

The world frowns if the bereaved forms a new relationship too soon, unless the former one was known to be unhappy or the new partner was already in place – in which case the world will have done its frowning already. A year's delay is traditional, although from the views expressed in this chapter above many survivors think this too soon. There are more important reasons for not jumping straightaway than what other people think. Rebound relationships generally have poor prospects.

Above all, the bereaved may have to work through feelings of betraying the previous partner. Even if they know it's what the departed would have wanted for them, their children may not see it that way. Nor do most people want to cut links with the dead one's relations, and fear possible problems from the late partner's parents or siblings. Evidence from the agony columns suggests that these families usually come round in the end. They want the surviving partner to be happy.

Lightning flashed for Nancy Whelan and Martin Preston when they met in the days before the Second World War. The well favoured couple – she a pretty red-headed amateur actress, he an Oxford undergraduate with a sports car – embarked on an idyllic romance amid the beauties of the Chiltern Hills. Its ardour is captured in surviving letters*.

He wrote: 'You turn me so inside out – no one has ever done it before … you leave me breathless … You are the most exciting thing in the world … your love is like a crown. If I could be with you right now I would frighten you with my passion. I can't say more – you must feel it.' She wrote: 'I think of you day and night. The moment I open my eyes in the morning. And when I close them at night. Your love lifts me up. It's a crown I wear in my heart.'

*Reported by the *Daily Mail* and quoted in *The Very White of Love,* by S.C. Worrall (Nancy's son), a fictionalised retelling of their romance.

Their love affair was overtaken by the war. Martin died in action soon after the start, in 1940. A grief-stricken Nancy kept his picture on her dressing table to the end of her life sixty-five years later. Her sorrow was perhaps made worse by the fact that she hadn't known Martin in the fullest sense. Unlike many others in wartime the couple decided to stay chaste until marriage, although Nancy was later to rail against the 'false morality of the times'.

Six years later, as most did in the same situation, she found someone else in place of her lost love. She married Philip Worrall, a handsome war hero, and went on to have three sons. The couple were 'madly in love', Nancy's son Simon told the *Daily Mail*. She was fortunate that she had a man who was 'secure enough' – Simon's words – to accept that picture of Martin on the dressing table (where there were also pictures of her husband and sons).

Whether or not lightning struck twice for Nancy, for all of us contentment is in plentiful supply.

After death or divorce, social life may take a dive. Dinner party invitations dry up unless the singleton can be of use as a plus-one. Anyone ready to take on the challenges – and satisfactions – of holidaying alone encounters the often-steep single-room supplements. The wish to resume a sex life is the least of the reasons for forming a new relationship given the ready availability of sex for singles (known as joining a library rather than buying the book). But fears prey on older people who live alone. We worry about how long we will be capable of looking after the house and perhaps a garden, or how long we may lie ill or dead before someone knows about it. Truly, the world is arranged for couples. However, re-partnering should be more than merely defensive. If we're lucky, we'll discover that rainbows do end and love does come along for a second time.

PUBLICATION DATA

© Martin Horrocks, 2018
The moral rights of the author have been asserted

Cover picture, courtesy of Wikimedia Commons, shows Elizabeth and Darcy from Jane Austen's *Pride and Prejudice* (1813), drawn by Hugh Thomson and published in 1894. [This drawing is in the public domain in the United Kingdom, the United States and other countries and areas where the copyright term is the author's life plus 70 years or less]

A Horse Without a Carriage: Love and Marriage Through the Ages
published 2018 by
Edge Editions
Kings Nympton
Umberleigh EX37 9ST (UK)

ISBN 9780992965853

www.ituri.co.uk

Printed in the UK by 4edge Ltd
www.4edge.co.uk

All rights reserved. No part of this publication may be reproduced, stored in a retrieval system, or transmitted in any form or by any means (electronic, mechanical, photocopying, recording or otherwise) without the prior written permission of the publisher

AKNOWLEDGEMENT

The author acknowledges his debt to Wikipedia, an invaluable fount of essential information. The publisher, Edge Editions, actively supports the not-for-profit Wikipedia Foundation, which welcomes donations, small or large, to further the work of the free online encyclopaedia in many languages: www.wikipedia.org/

IF YOU LIKED this mini-book you may wish to read Martin Horrocks's *Everyman and the Beautiful People* – the three parts of his romantic novel sequence brought together in a single volume. Available from Amazon as a Kindle ebook. Some individual parts are still available also in a printed version from www.ituri.co.uk (*Girl at the Top Table*, ebook only – print sold out; *His Lordship's Disgraceful Daughter*, ebook and print; *Coda for a Star*, ebook and print).